UNSUNG WEILL

UNSUNG WEILL

22 Songs
Cut from Broadway Shows and Hollywood Films

Edited by Elmar Juchem

EUROPEAN AMERICAN MUSIC CORPORATION

Piano parts of the following songs edited by Thomas Rosenkranz: "Street Light Is My Moonlight," "Love in a Mist,"
"Bats about You," "Unforgettable," "Too Much to Dream," "The Picture on the Wall."

Photo Credits:
Weill-Lenya Research Center (frontispiece, 8, 58, 65, 79);
Photofest (40, 74); The New York Public Library for the
Performing Arts, Billy Rose Theatre Collection (28)

Cover design and artwork by Alexandra Leff

EA-830   © 2002 by European American Music Corporation
All Rights Reserved   International Copyright Secured   Printed in U.S.A.

Non-dramatic public performances licensed through ASCAP
For dramatic performance rights, please contact the publisher

CONTENTS

INTRODUCTION

Rummaging around the cutting room floor of Kurt Weill's workshop is a fascinating experience. The various scraps of music range from barely legible pencil drafts to fully orchestrated versions complete with instrumental parts, mixed with heavily annotated lyric sheets from his collaborators. The material is not knee-deep, though. Cole Porter, for instance, routinely overwrote his shows, leaving it to the director to pick and choose. Not so Kurt Weill. The composer of the *Threepenny Opera* worked extremely economically and usually custom-tailored his music to the dramatic context. Yet this habit didn't prevent various pieces from being discarded.

Some of this wonderful material is now presented in this volume. In order to be included, songs had to be in a state of completeness that required no "recreative" editing and, equally important, they had to make sense without the story line for which they were intended. For those performers who want to know a little more about the original context of the songs, the following information may be helpful.

When Kurt Weill and Langston Hughes composed *Street Scene* in 1946, they had high hopes for **"Great Big Sky"** as it would have ended the first Act, sung by the janitor. Weill raved to his collaborator, "the song is a peach—and will be the most impressive act curtain, with a terrific lift at the end." But the role of the janitor was cut down as the show developed, and the song would have followed the big "Lilacs" duet. Hughes had a very specific notion when he drafted the lyrics for **"Street Light Is My Moonlight."** He visualized this number as a "nonchalant but very rhythmical jitterbug dance number" with "words you can spit out of the corner of your mouth in tough hilarity . . . 32 bar, two part (16-16) chorus, no verse needed for the show." Intended for the streetwise characters Mae and Dick, the song was dropped and replaced by the "less tough" dance number, "Moonfaced, Starry-Eyed," which focused on the couple rather than the city.

"You Understand Me So" sounds like a warm, joyful song (and can be sung as such), but in Alan Jay Lerner's libretto for *Love Life* (1948) it had a bitterly ironic taste, sung by an estranged husband and wife to people whom they have just met at a party onboard a cruise ship. The party scene had opened with the singer of the ship's band delivering the hilarious **"There's Nothing Left for Daddy (But the Rhumba)."** When Lerner revised the book, both songs were cut. A whole scene in a men's locker room was also dropped in Act II, and along with it went the patter song **"How I Love My Work,"** written for a slightly sadistic masseur who, according to Lerner's script, had "the girth of the Dome of St. Peter's."

One Touch of Venus (1943) underwent a major script change when Weill and Ogden Nash lost patience with their first choice of book author. In the course of rewriting, many songs had to be dropped, even though the authors tried to save some material in different contexts. **"Who Am I?"** was intended for a grumpy Vulcan, jealous of Venus. When the Mt. Olympus scene was cut, the song went into the opening of Act II to the art dealer Whitelaw Savory, terribly hungover and confused by a love interest. But the actor eventually cast for the role had a limited vocal ability. Venus would have sung **"Love in a Mist"** toward the end of the show, when her "owners" forced her to return in a downtown Manhattan waterfront scene, but the ending was rewritten. Another song from Mt. Olympus would have been **"Vive la différence,"** as the Gods observed human love.

In 1940, Weill collaborated with Ira Gershwin on *Lady in the Dark*. **"Bats about You"** was written to beef up the music of Act II. The song would have been sung during a flashback (Liza's high school graduation party) by her classmates, Ben ("the handsomest boy") and Barbara ("the most beautiful girl"). Gershwin envisaged the song in an "early Irving Berlin style" and even made up a fictitious show title ("Nay, Nay, Nellie"; 1922) from which the song was supposedly derived." **"Unforgettable"** would have been sung by Danny Kaye in the second dream of Act I, the Wedding Dream. In this sequence, Kaye was supposed to be a movie director teaching a movie star how to perform the number. The lyrics for **"It's Never Too Late to Mendelssohn,"** also intended for Kaye in the Wedding Dream, are packed with allusions. They poke fun at the two best-known pieces of wedding music, Felix Mendelssohn's "Wedding March" from *A Midsummer Night's Dream* and Richard Wagner's "Bridal Chorus" from *Lohengrin*. Today, many of the references are rather obscure, such as George Jean Nathan, famed theater critic for *Newsweek*, *Esquire* and other popular magazines, and his colleague Burns Mantle, first-stringer for the *New York Daily News*. "Mischa" and "Jascha" (pronounced: YA-sha) were the two virtuoso violinists, Mischa Elman and Jascha Heifetz, and "a play by Bernstein" alludes to the French playwright Henri Bernstein, whose plays *Mélo* and *Promise* featured love triangles and ran on Broadway in the 1930s. The song was dropped but a few lines survived, rhythmically spoken by the character Charley Johnson. **"It Could Have Happened to Anyone"** was written with Gershwin for the film *Where Do We Go from Here?* (1945) in which the protagonist, played by comedian Fred MacMurray, is a bit of a loser and his girlfriend wonders why she fell in love with him. It's not clear why this excellent song was cut.

Playwright Maxwell Anderson worked with Weill on two shows. **"How Far Will You Go with Me?"** was written for the second act of *Knickerbocker Holiday* (1938), where the show's ingenue, Tina Tienhoven, tries to make up an excuse so the tyrannical New Amsterdam governor Peter Stuyvesant, played by Walter Huston, won't hang her boyfriend. This entire scene was cut. *Lost in the Stars*, the 1949 "musical tragedy" set in apartheid South Africa, had a meditative song, **"The Little Tin God,"** after the first scene. The number was intended as commentary by the Leader of the Chorus, but it was cut when material was needed for the show's star, Todd Duncan, and a new song was composed.

For the Fritz Lang movie *You and Me* (1938), Weill had many ideas about turning it into a "musical film" but not a film musical. The studio's initial response was positive, but when the film reached the dubbing stage the concept had changed and most songs were cut. Two victims of this decision are the hilarious **"Too Much to Dream,"** a terrific hangover song starting "out of tune" on the 7th degree of the scale, and the speculative, woeful **"The Romance of a Lifetime."**

The situation is less clear for the songs with lyrics by Ann Ronell. Weill worked with her on two movies, *The River Is Blue* (1937–38) and the screen adaptation of *One Touch of Venus* for Ava Gardner (1948), but **"The Picture on the Wall"** and **"Your Technique"** cannot be conclusively linked to either project. Judging from the paper and the handwriting, they were probably written in the late 1930s. **"The River Is So Blue"** would have been the title song of their first known collaboration, but the producer replaced, one by one, director, screenwriter, and finally score.

Oscar Hammerstein wrote the lyric to **"The Good Earth"** in February 1942. He and Weill intended to use the song for a film, most likely a propaganda film, as this song clearly belongs into the World War II period. Technically speaking, **"Inventory"** is not a cut song, in that it was performed in *Lunchtime Follies*, an entertainment program for workers in war-related industries. The text is by Lewis Allan (aka Abel Meeropol), who is best known for authoring the song "Strange Fruit," made famous by Billie Holiday. **"Farewell, Goodbye"** would have been part of *Johnny Johnson* (1936), when Minnie Belle parts from Johnny in Act I as he is sent off to a military training camp and on to Europe in WW I turmoil.

Songs for musicals get cut for many reasons: book revisions, lack of finances, vocal limitations of stars, overall length of a show. Sometimes the song just doesn't work as intended. Rarely, in Weill's case, was a song not up to standards. I hope the twenty-two rarities made available here will enrich the repertory of Weill's American songs and that performers will enjoy and polish these gems.

Elmar Juchem

Langston Hughes

Great Big Sky

Lyrics by
LANGSTON HUGHES

Music by
KURT WEILL

Moderato assai

It's a great big sky And there's room en-ough for all Un-der-

neath the great big sky Where the earth's a lit - tle ball And a man ain't much But

yet a man is all That stands up tall Be - tween the earth and God be -

neath the Great Big Sky.

The fish in the sea, The birds that fly, The el - e - phants and bees Are

all part of the why, That great big why That keeps a man a-wonder-in'

All night long a-wonder-in', A - fret-tin' and a-wonder-in' Be - neath the Great Big

12

Street Light Is My Moonlight

Lyrics by
LANGSTON HUGHES

Music by
KURT WEILL

Jitterbug (very rhythmical, not too fast)

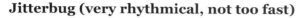

He: The street light is my
street light is our
street light is my
street light is my

moon - light, hon - ey babe.___ The
moon - light, hon - ey babe.___ Two
moon - light, hon - ey babe.___ **She:** Tall
moon - light, hon - ey babe.___ **She:** The

14

Street Light Is My Moonlight - 3 - 2

Street Light Is My Moonlight - 3 - 3

You Understand Me So

Lyrics by
ALAN JAY LERNER

Music by
KURT WEILL

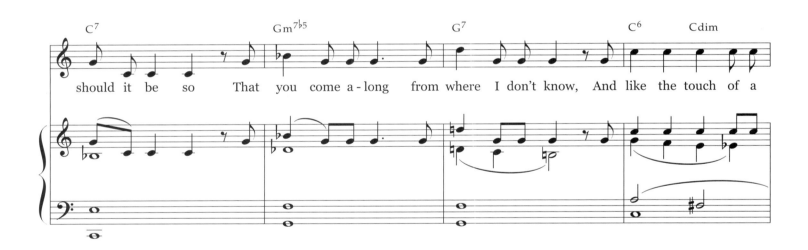

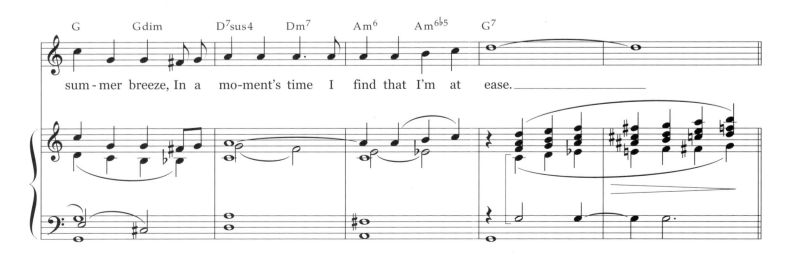

There's Nothing Left for Daddy
(But the Rhumba)

Lyrics by
ALAN JAY LERNER

Music by
KURT WEILL

So when you see him danc-ing by,_____

Re - mem - ber there's a rea - son why._____

Tempo di Rhumba

There's

noth - ing left for dad - dy but the rhum - ba._____ There's

There's Nothing Left for Daddy (But the Rhumba) - 9 - 3

not an-oth-er thing he'd rath-er do._____ For

dad-dy's aw-ful glad he found the rhum-ba;_____ The

rhum-ba makes him feel like twen-ty - two._____ So

ev'-ry time they play a La-tin num-ber_____ Then

24

There's Nothing Left for Daddy (But the Rhumba) - 9 - 6

There's Nothing Left for Daddy (But the Rhumba) - 9 - 9

Kurt Weill & Alan Jay Lerner

How I Love My Work

(The Masseur's Song from the "Locker Room Scene")

Lyrics by
ALAN JAY LERNER

Music by
KURT WEILL

Who Am I?

Lyrics by
OGDEN NASH

Music by
KURT WEILL

Moderato (Boogie-Woogie Tempo)

How do I feel to-day?

I feel a-bom-i-na-ble, And it is the re-

34

sult of dis-tur-ban-ces psy - chi-at-ric rath-er than ab - dom-i - na - ble.

Who am I an - y - way, a God or mere-ly a

ge - nius? I am a - wear - y of be-ing schiz-o -

phren - ius. ___ Is there

Who Am I? - 7 - 2

an - y-one___ in the house who would care for an ex-tra i-den - ti - ty?___ I've got plen - ti - ty!___

The time has come___ ___ to face re-al - i -ties Just be-cause I have per-son - al - i - ty e-nough for two does-n't

38

39

Who Am I? - 7 - 7

Ogden Nash

Love in a Mist

Lyrics by
OGDEN NASH

Music by
KURT WEILL

I'd nev-er heard of love in a mist,_ No warn-ing word of love in a mist,_

I don't know why or how I'm lost, But now I'm lost In love in a mist._

Vive la différence

Lyrics by
OGDEN NASH

Music by
KURT WEILL

He takes a show-er, Then
He likes to lin-ger For__

__ a has-ty rub. She takes an ho-ur Soak-ing in the tub. *Vive la dif-fér-*
__ an-oth-er scotch. She keeps her fin-ger Point-ing at her watch.

en- ce!
He leaves ath-let-ics to__
He's so re-morse-ful Ev'-

Bats about You

Lyrics by
IRA GERSHWIN

Music by
KURT WEILL

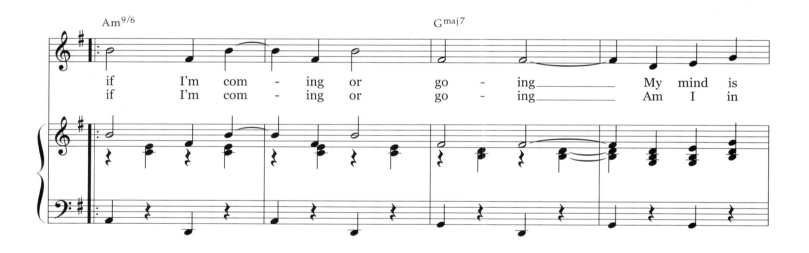

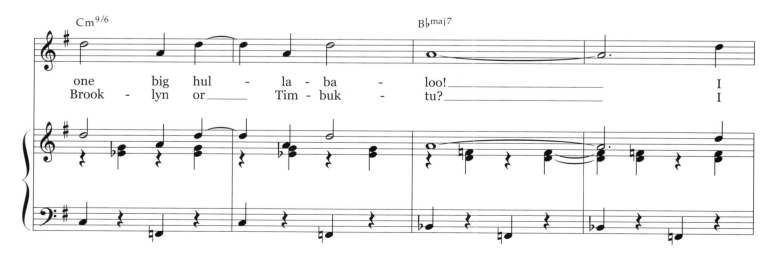

Unforgettable

Lyrics by
IRA GERSHWIN

Music by
KURT WEILL

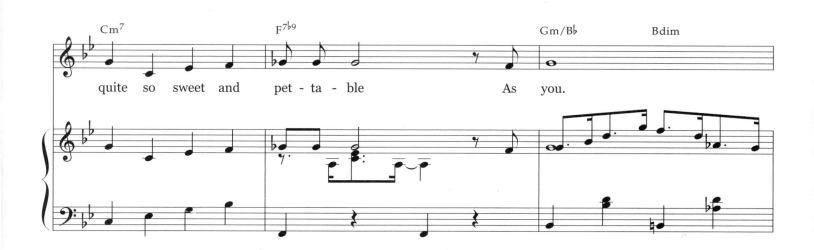

52

Unforgettable - 3 - 2

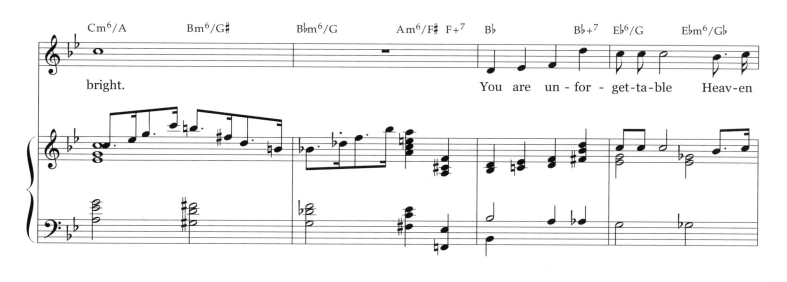

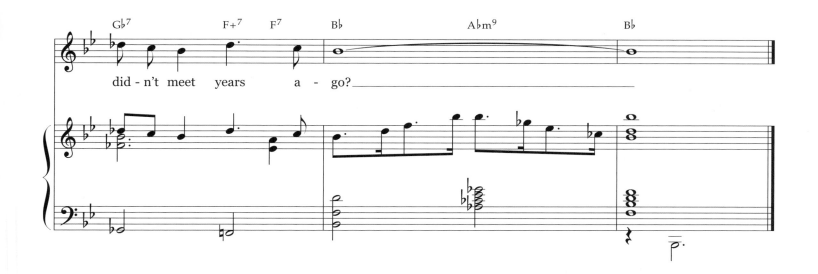

It's Never Too Late to Mendelssohn

Lyrics by
IRA GERSHWIN

Music by
KURT WEILL

It's Never Too Late to Mendelssohn - 4 - 3

Ira Gershwin

It Could Have Happened to Anyone

Lyrics by
IRA GERSHWIN

Music by
KURT WEILL

Lightly, but not too fast

He's no col-lec-tion Of man-ly per-fec-tion Oth-er girls find him ex-pend-a-ble. Of love I'm a vic-tim, For my heart has picked him And my heart is de-pend-a-ble. When I

How Far Will You Go with Me?

Lyrics by
MAXWELL ANDERSON

Music by
KURT WEILL

64

How Far Will You Go with Me? - 3 - 3

Kurt Weill & Maxwell Anderson

The Little Tin God

Lyrics by
MAXWELL ANDERSON

Music by
KURT WEILL

68

The Little Tin God - 3 - 3

YOU AND ME

Too Much to Dream

Lyrics by
SAM COSLOW

Music by
KURT WEILL

Too Much to Dream - 3 - 3

The Romance of a Lifetime

Lyrics by
SAM COSLOW

Music by
KURT WEILL

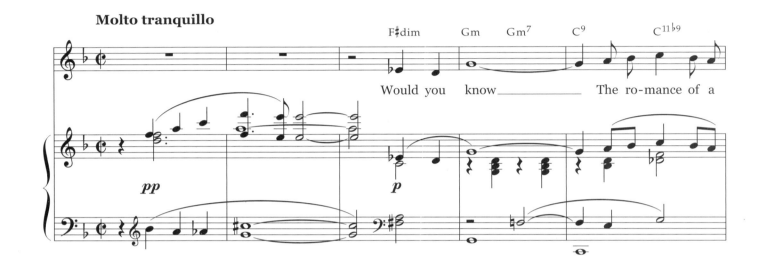

Molto tranquillo

Would you know____ The ro-mance of a

life - time____ Would you sense it____ When you met face to face?____

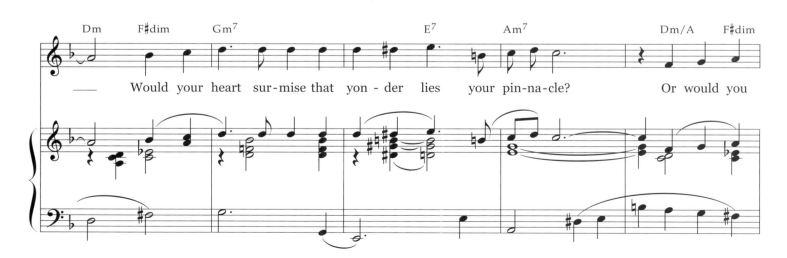

Would your heart sur-mise that yon - der lies your pin-na-cle?____ Or would you

Sam Coslow

The Picture on the Wall

Lyrics by
ANN RONELL

Music by
KURT WEILL

Moderato

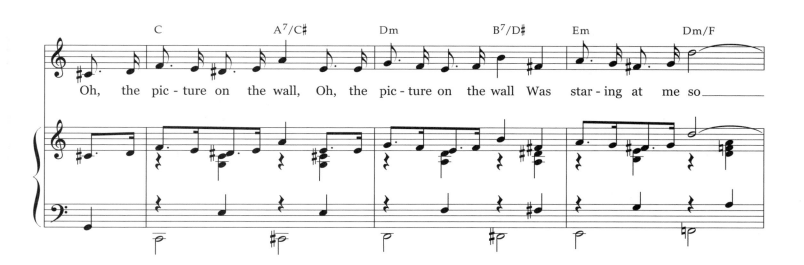

Oh, the pic-ture on the wall, Oh, the pic-ture on the wall Was star-ing at me so

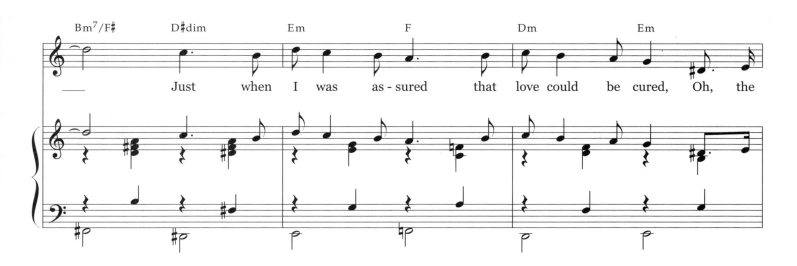

Just when I was as-sured that love could be cured, Oh, the

76

The Picture on the Wall - 4 - 2

Ann Ronell

Your Technique

Lyrics by
ANN RONELL

Music by
KURT WEILL

The River Is So Blue

Lyrics by
ANN RONELL

Music by
KURT WEILL

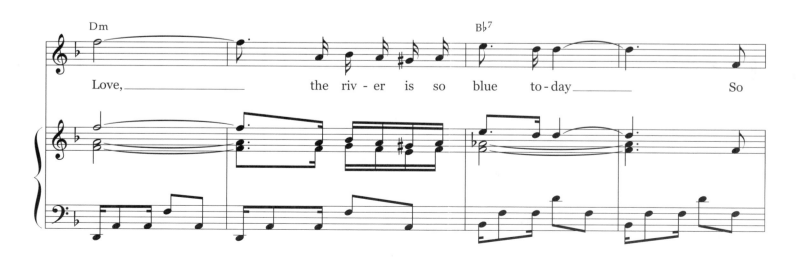

The River Is So Blue - 4 - 2

The Good Earth

Lyrics by
OSCAR HAMMERSTEIN II

Music by
KURT WEILL

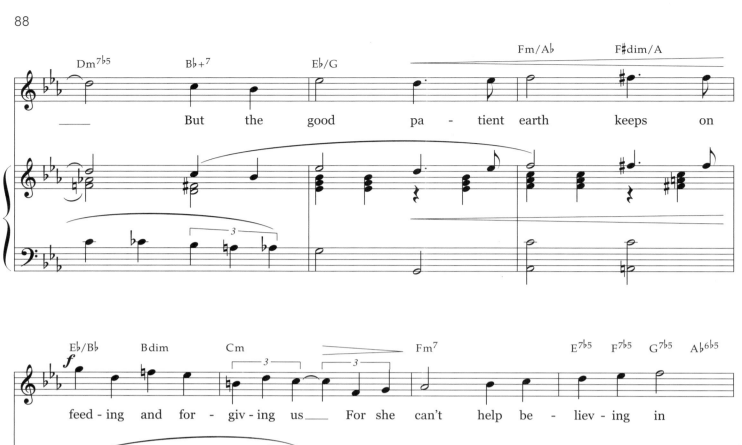

But the good pa - tient earth keeps on

feed - ing and for - giv - ing us____ For she can't help be - liev - ing in

man.____

Inventory

Lyrics by
LEWIS ALLAN

Music by
KURT WEILL

Alternative lyrics written
for a performance at an oil
refinery
("A" sections only):

A thousand planes
  are off today,
High octane gas
  is on its way,
A thousand pilots
  shout "Hooray!" for
The man who held the rod
That placed the weld
That made the seam
That sealed the plate
That formed the shell
That made the "cat"
That fueled the plane
That held the bomb
That dropped on Hitler.

A thousand bombers
  for the Yanks,
A million gallons
  in their tanks,
High octane gas
  is working thanks to
The man who held the rod
That placed the weld
That made the seam
That sealed the plate
That formed the shell
That made the "cat"
That fueled the plane
That held the bomb
That dropped on Hitler.

When bombers roar
  and cannons blaze,
When bombs go flying
  from the bays,
When men pass
  ammunition praise
The man who held the rod
That placed the weld
That made the seam
That sealed the plate
That formed the shell
That made the "cat"
That fueled the plane
That held the bomb
That dropped on Hitler.

Farewell, Goodbye

Lyrics by
PAUL GREEN

Music by
KURT WEILL

Fare-well, good-bye,_ Good-bye, fare-well,_ I

have no words my love to tell, fare-well. A - lone I'll wait_ Stead-fast and true,_ My

ev' - ry thought A thought of you, of you._ So go, my dear, and quick-ly now, And

then the cru-el deed is done, For part-ing is a shar-per blow Than ab-sence, my be-lov-ed one. Good-

bye, fare-well,___ Fare-well, good-bye,___ For nev-er maid did love as I, good-

bye! A-lone I wait, stead-fast and true,___ my ev'-ry thought a

thought of you, of you of you.___

Farewell, Goodbye - 2 - 2